Published in 2022 by Groundwood Books / House of Anansi Press
groundwoodbooks.com
Second printing 2024

We gratefully acknowledge for their financial support of our publishing program
the Canada Council for the Arts, the Ontario Arts Council and the Government
of Canada.

With the participation of the Government of Canada
Avec la participation du gouvernement du Canada | Canadä

Library and Archives Canada Cataloguing in Publication
Title: West Coast wild at low tide / words by Deborah Hodge ; pictures by Karen
Reczuch. Other titles: At low tide
Names: Hodge, Deborah, author. | Reczuch, Karen, illustrator.
Identifiers: Canadiana (print) 20210233087 | Canadiana (ebook) 20210233273
| ISBN 9781773064130 (hardcover) | ISBN 9781773064147 (EPUB) | ISBN
9781773064154 (Kindle)
Subjects: LCSH: Coastal animals—British Columbia—Pacific Coast—Juvenile
literature. | LCSH: Coastal animals—British Columbia—Pacific Coast—Pictorial
works—Juvenile literature. | LCSH: Coastal ecology—British Columbia—Pacific
Coast—Juvenile literature. | LCSH: Coastal ecology—British Columbia—Pacific
Coast—Pictorial works—Juvenile literature.
Classification: LCC QL221.B7 H63 2022 | DDC j591.9711/1—dc23

The illustrations were done in watercolor and color pencil.
Edited by Emma Sakamoto
Designed by Michael Solomon
Printed and bound in China

WEST
COAST
WILD
AT LOW TIDE

In memory of my dad, Lyndon Grove,
a true wordsmith and gracious
literary mentor
—DH

For Elliot — and a lifetime of
sharing discovery and exploration
— KR

WEST COAST WILD

AT LOW TIDE

WORDS BY

DEBORAH HODGE

PICTURES BY

KAREN RECZUCH

GROUNDWOOD BOOKS

HOUSE OF ANANSI PRESS

TORONTO / BERKELEY

At the edge of the majestic ocean, on the Pacific west coast, endless tides shift back and forth, twice every day. The ocean is always moving, drawn by the forces of the moon and sun.

At high tide, the sea is near, splashing over the rocks and sand. At low tide, the ocean retreats and a beautiful beach is revealed.

Between the ebb and flow of the tides lies the intertidal zone, where a remarkable community of creatures thrives in a home of ever-changing conditions.

Ochre Sea Star

Brightly colored sea stars often live in tidepools
— small pools of water left in hollow spots as the
tide recedes. A sea star crawls on tiny tube feet
to hunt mussels, barnacles and snails. If one of
its arms is torn off by a hungry gull, it will grow
a new one! Sea stars soak up water, tuck into a
crevice or move down to keep from drying out at
low tide.

Giant Green Anemone

The giant green anemone looks like an underwater flower, but it is an animal, not a plant. Its wavy tentacles sting and paralyze the crabs, fish and other creatures that swim or crawl by. Then the tentacles pull the captured prey into the anemone's mouth to be digested. When the tide is low, anemones fold up their bodies to keep moist and cool.

Blueband Hermit Crab

A hermit crab carries an empty snail shell wherever it goes. This sturdy home protects its soft body. Hermit crabs scurry through tidepools, where water almost always covers them. If predators approach, the little crab slips deep inside the shell and blocks the opening with its large claw. It will trade its shell for a bigger one as it grows.

Sea Lemon

A sea lemon gives off a strong fruity scent. Its coloring warns fish and other creatures to stay away! Its favorite food is the bread-crumb sponge, often yellow-colored too. The sea lemon eats by scraping up pieces of the sponge with its rough tongue called a radula. These colorful sea slugs are often found tucked under seaweed.

Giant Pacific Octopus

This graceful creature is the largest octopus in the world! It changes its skin color and texture to blend in with its surroundings and hide from predators. The octopus streaks though the water, hunting crabs, clams and other shellfish with its long arms and powerful suction cups. At low tide, it can squeeze into a crevice in the rocks.

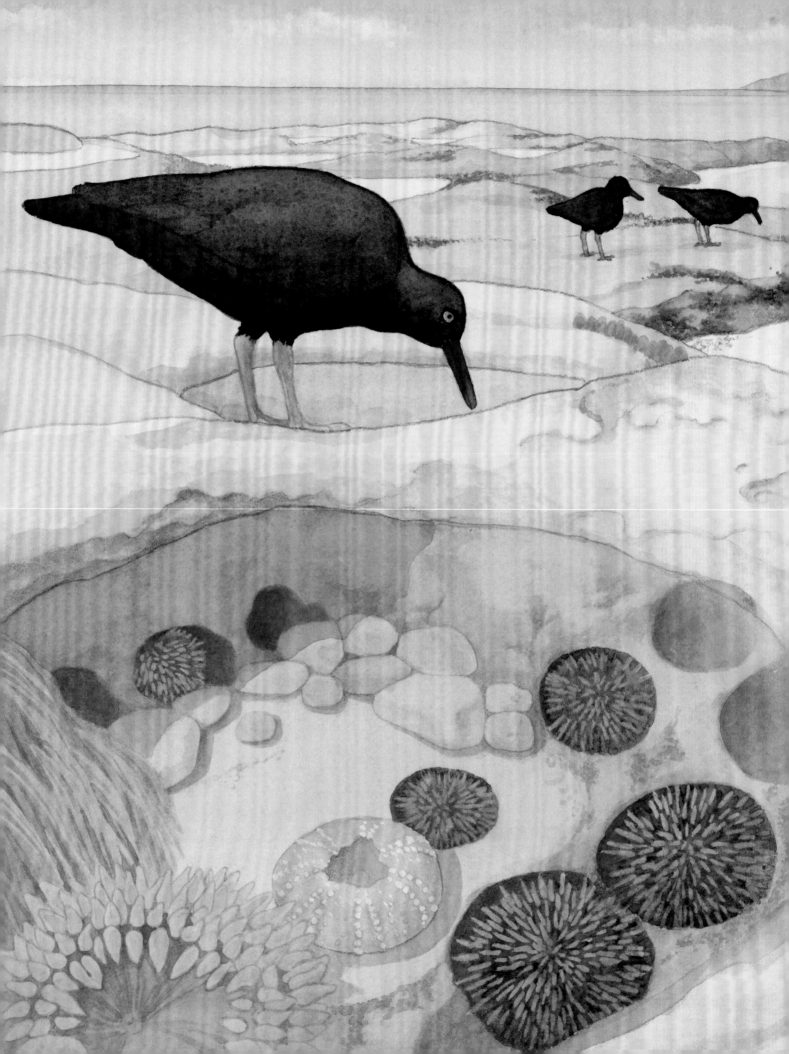

Purple Sea Urchin

Vibrant purple sea urchins can burrow into soft rock with their five sharp teeth, chewing up algae and even eating the rock. Nestling into a pit may help protect an urchin from predators and allow it to hold on in a pounding surf. Its long pointy spines keep some hungry animals away, but many urchins are devoured by sea otters.

Giant Red Sea Cucumber

This eye-catching creature crawls along the seabed on its tube feet and uses clusters of sticky white tentacles near its mouth to mop up food, usually dead or decaying matter. At low tide, it pulls in its tentacles. If a predator is hunting it, the sea cucumber can push out its organs and leave them behind as a substitute meal. It will grow new ones later.

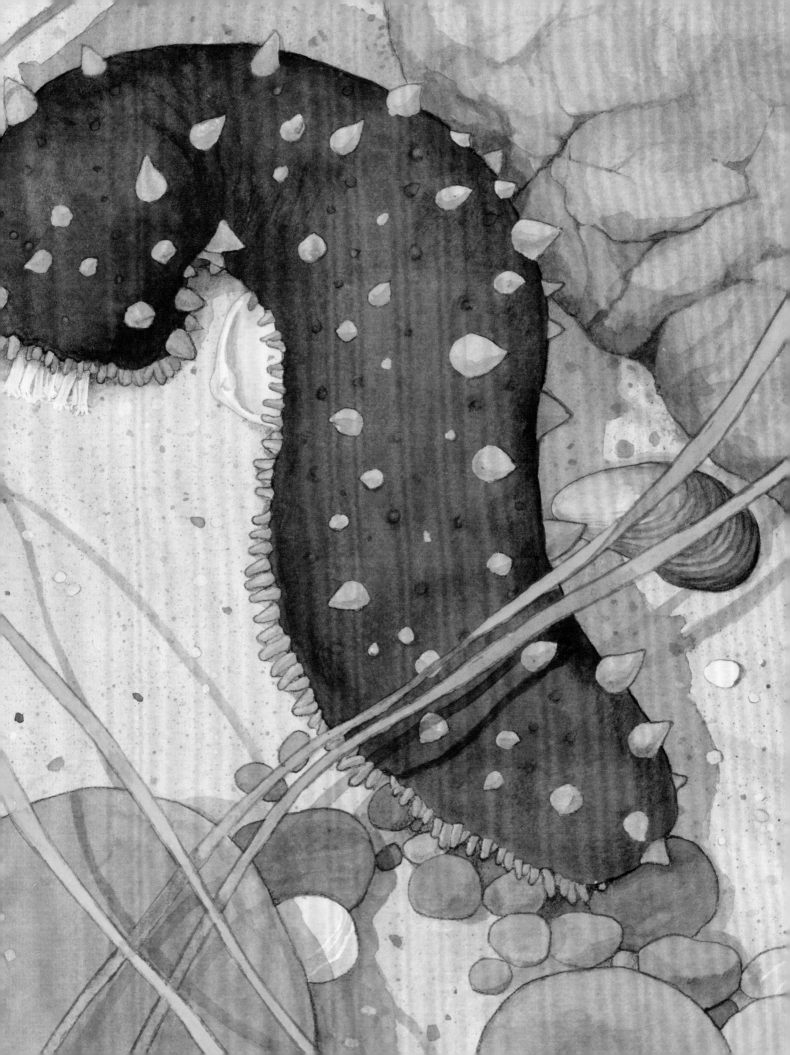

Sand Dollar

A sand dollar burrows into the sand just below the low tide line, and eats plankton and sand. The heavy grains weigh it down so the waves can't easily carry it out to sea. A sand dollar has dark fuzzy spines for feeding and moving, and tiny pincers for catching plankton. When it dies, only its pale, hollow shell with a delicate flower pattern remains.

Pacific Blue Mussel

Mussels anchor themselves to rocks with strong, silky fibers called byssal threads. The threads help secure them in a crashing surf. Mussels are a favorite food of crabs, birds and sea stars. At high tide, mussels open their beautiful blue shells to take in food and oxygen. As the water recedes, they close, keeping a bit of the ocean inside.

Whitecap Limpet

A soft-bodied sea snail lives inside this pointed shell. The limpet has a strong, muscular foot that clings to rocks, making it hard for the tide to wash it away. The snail scrapes up food with its raspy tongue. Its white shell is often covered by the bumpy pink algae that it eats!

Penpoint Gunnel

This long, slender fish swims like an eel, twisting and swaying through a tidepool or low intertidal area. The gunnel's color helps it stay camouflaged. Brown gunnels hide in brown kelp, while red ones stay in red seaweed, and green fish find cover in sea lettuce or eelgrass. When a gunnel is out of water, it can breathe air.

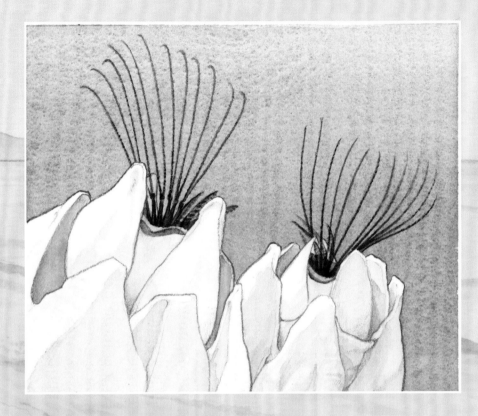

Acorn Barnacle

A barnacle glues itself to a rock with a very strong cement. As the tide washes over it, the hard shell opens and feathery little feet, called cirri, come out to catch tiny floating plants and animals. When the tide recedes, this shrimp-like creature closes up its shell, capturing the food and water it needs until the waves return once more.

Bat Star

Bat stars have webbing between their arms, like a bat's wing. These colorful sea stars are often found in shallow sandy or muddy areas, or in eelgrass meadows. A bat star feeds on dead animals and algae, helping to clean up the ocean floor. It eats by pushing its stomach over the food and digesting it outside its body before absorbing it.

Tidepool Sculpin

These little fish change color to match their
surroundings and help them hide from diving
birds or other predators. They easily adapt to
shifting temperatures — from cool water at high
tide to the warmth of shallow, sunny tidepools
at low tide. If a sculpin is moved from its home
area, it can find its way back using its keen sense
of smell.

Every day on this wild west coast, a spectacular array of creatures is living in rhythm with the tides and thriving at the ocean's edge.

When the tide is low, and the sea retreats, the shoreline animals have ways of staying cool and moist, finding food, and hiding from the hungry predators that prowl the beautiful beach.

When the tide is high, and the waves return, the ocean brings food, oxygen and cover, allowing the intertidal creatures to open up and move freely once more.

THE WEST COAST INTERTIDAL ZONE

The Pacific west coast is a magnificent area with an abundance of marine life, flourishing in the intertidal zone — a narrow strip of beach situated between the high and low tide lines. Here the tides cross back and forth twice a day, pulled by the gravitational forces of the moon and sun.

It is a challenging environment, where its inhabitants must constantly adapt to the changing tides. The intertidal animals are sometimes covered by salty seawater and other times exposed to sun, wind, freshwater rain or freezing temperatures.

Some experience crashing waves, then quiet tidepools; or are exposed on rocky shores and then covered; or are concealed from land predators and then in full view.

Many of the creatures in this book are commonly found on the coast from northern California to western Alaska, with British Columbia, Washington and Oregon in between. Sheltered bays with lightly sloping rocky shores and tidepools are often a good place to spot them, especially in the two hours before and after the lowest tide of the day.

Beachcombers should strive to be gentle and not disturb the animals in their fragile seaside homes. When exploring the seashore, it is crucial to check tide times and keep a close watch on the ocean (never turning your back on it), to avoid being swept off rocks or stranded from shore in a rising tide. Children should always be accompanied by an adult.

The Pacific west coast has vast stretches of pristine wilderness, some of the last remaining temperate rainforests in the world, and an extraordinary community of ocean creatures and marine life. This awe-inspiring region, with its bountiful intertidal species, plays a vital role in our ecosystem and is important to preserve.

For Further Exploration

West Coast Aquariums
Discover more about the intertidal creatures in this book by visiting, online or in person, one of the many wonderful aquariums along the Pacific west coast. Look for aquariums in Vancouver and Ucluelet, BC; Seattle, WA; Newport, OR; and San Francisco, Monterey and Long Beach, CA.

Websites
Pacific Rim National Park Reserve
Explore the breathtakingly beautiful marine and temperate rainforest region on the west coast of Vancouver Island, British Columbia: pc.gc.ca/en/pn-np/bc/pacificrim/

Learn more about the intertidal zone: pc.gc.ca/en/pn-np/bc/pacificrim/nature/littoral-marin-shoreline

Books
Curious Kids Nature Guide: Explore the Amazing Outdoors of the Pacific Northwest by Fiona Cohen, illustrated by Marni Fylling, Little Bigfoot – Sasquatch Books, 2017

The New Beachcomber's Guide to the Pacific Northwest by J. Duane Sept, Harbour Publishing, 2019

One Small Place by the Sea by Barbara Brenner, illustrated by Tom Leonard, HarperCollins, 2004

Star of the Sea: A Day in the Life of a Starfish by Janet Halfmann, illustrated by Joan Paley, Henry Holt, 2011

A Walk on the Beach: Into the Field Guide by Laurie Goldman, Downtown Bookworks, 2013

West Coast Wild: A Nature Alphabet by Deborah Hodge, illustrated by Karen Reczuch, Groundwood Books, 2015

Acknowledgments

My deep gratitude to the many people who helped bring this book to life! Thank you especially to Adrienne Mason, biologist, writer and managing editor of *Hakai Magazine: Coastal Science and Societies*, Tofino, BC. Adrienne's expertise in reviewing both art and text, and her understanding of west coast creatures and ecosystems, was invaluable. Thank you also to Meghan Warren and Laurie Filgiano of the Ucluelet Aquarium for generously sharing their knowledge of intertidal animals. To Karen Reczuch, for her gorgeous art and creative partnership; to Emma Sakamoto, our esteemed editor, for always keeping us on track; and to Michael Solomon, art director, and his design team, for beautiful pages. Karen Reczuch and I are grateful to publisher Karen Li and the entire Groundwood staff for their dedication in creating quality books for children, and for their faith in our work. Thank you, all!